The Tao of
Programming

The Tao of Programming

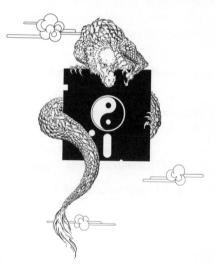

GEOFFREY JAMES

Library of Congress Cataloging-in-Publication Data

James, Geoffrey, 1953-
　The tao of programming.

　1. Electronic digital computers--Programming--
Anecdotes, facetiae, satire, etc. I. Title.
Qa76.6.J354　1986　　　005　　　86-18635
ISBN 0-931137-07-1

Cover design and illustration: Gloria Garland
Text design and illustrations: Gloria Garland

Published in the United States of America

10 9 8 7 6 5 4 3 2 1

ISBN 0-931137-07-1

INFO
BOOKS

P.O. BOX 1018
SANTA MONICA
CALIFORNIA 90406

For my friend, John L. Joseph, who provided much of the inspiration for this book.

00101100

Frontispiece

Ancient likeness of the ninth immortal of computer programming. He is shown with the traditional lotus (which symbolizes project planning), crane (assembly code), jackal (job control language), and floppy disk (file management system). He is suspended between earth and sky, meditating on the contents of the cosmic Q-Register. Above him are pictured flitting bats, which represent the distractions of the material world. Below him, the primordial dragon of chaos gives birth to the mystery of Tao.

Preface

The field of compuarcheology is sufficiently new that even an amateur like myself can sometimes stumble upon significant discoveries. Several years ago, as I was making a somewhat desultory search through a pile of obsolete punch cards, I discovered what appeared to be a set of coded bit-map images. The images were sandwiched among thousands of obsolete RPG programs and I wouldn't have given them a second glance if it hadn't been for a hand-written note on one of the cards saying: "Destroy after processing."

This quite naturally piqued my interest
and I was determined to discover the
contents of the mysterious card pack. It
was clear from the first that the images
had been scrambled and encrypted, but
with perseverence (as well as hundreds
of hours of raw CPU time), I was finally able to produce a rough outline of
the first image, which is reproduced at
the beginning of Book One.

But the decryption of the images turned
out to be the simplest part of the project.
The manuscript was in an unfamiliar
dialect and had to be transcribed before
any realistic translation could be at-
tempted. As this effort proceeded, it

became clear to me that I was dealing
not with a simple set of test images (as
I had originally believed), but the legen-
dary "Tao of Programming" itself.

It is difficult to describe my excitement
at this revelation. Though I had certainly heard of the "Tao of Programming", I had never seen a copy of the
work nor met anybody who possessed
one. I had heard many times about how
the "Tao of Programming" had a profound, if covert, effect upon the early
development of computers. According
to these legends, the "Tao of Programming" represented the first attempt to
treat the art of programming as an

organic whole. As such it was vio-
lently opposed by both the academic
and business communities, who viewed
it as a threat to the established order of
things. The "Tao of Programming"
was forced underground, circulating
among select programmers and then
only after rigorous initiations.

Eventually, this so-called "Integration
Sect" became so powerful that it could
no longer remain clandestine. The
persecutions that followed (often re-
ferred to as "The Great Lay-Off") re-
sulted not only in the destruction of the
sect but (it was assumed) the loss of

the esoteric literature that comprised
the sect's inner teachings.

The truth in these legends is impossible
to verify and thus should be discounted
as mere colorful tales, more the prov-
ince of the anthropologist than the serious compuarcheologist. But now that
a manuscript has finally surfaced, it
may be possible to separate the truth
from the myth.

The origins of the "Tao of Programming" are lost in the mists of time.
From internal references we know that
certain passages can be dated from after
the invention of the integrated circuit.
But more accurate placing of the work

will have to wait until the full force of scholarship has been turned upon this hitherto-unknown classic.

The authorship of the "Tao of Programming" also remains a mystery. Tradition assigns certain portions of the text to Yong Yo Sef of the Sixth See Pee dynasty. Other scholars (I shall name no names) have somehow managed to conclude that the work is a mere compilation of tales whose authorship can never be determined. However, all agree that the profundity of the work is clearly of such magnitude that the existence of the author is a trivial issue at best.

Perhaps these controversies can be cleared up now that the "Tao of Programming" is about to be published. If so, then the effort that I have put into preparing the manuscript will not have been in vain. However, I must confess that it is with some hesitation that I put forward a translation of this classic. All translations are by definition interpretive, and the flavor of the original can only be echoed faintly and never reproduced in its full richness.

The question has occasionally come up concerning my own beliefs. I hereby state unequivocally that while I respect the tradition that the "Tao of Programming" represents, I would never adhere to the more radical doctrines that it con-

tains. In particular, I find the attitude of
the text to management and corporations
completely reprehensible, though perhaps understandable given the political
climate of the times.

With no further ado or further non-ado,
I present my humble rendition of the
"Tao of Programming". Those who
understand the true nature of Tao will,
I trust, be amused by my presumption.

Geoffrey James
Los Angeles, 1986

Table of Contents

八晨　韶主　　　　　九　寒

飛生　總獸　　　攝精　川都

上靈　　　境之　馥　　　空　輪　灌

黃　　雲運　神　　開　　　　沃

華　玄明　君川　廓キ

延　丹　淨密　四　六　　十有

宛庭　　方　律　　　　十六

出五　　　　　　三門

THE
SILENT
VOID

Book One

単傾代亜低傾仕供合人作供亜供値仕価何

何余余供全側化価何側値偏何供作値何余

供値位余値係

Thus spake the master programmer:

"When you have learned to snatch the error code from the trap frame, it will be time for you to leave."

低人位仕位
偏他仕供曲
何何低合年
低位代人全
代全人作側
供側係供他
全傾余三低
傾仕位何仕
值価合係值
供何人再何
価低体係全
供全合位今
三何何係
值仕不何
位位全仕
低余作全
人值余作
仕位合全

1.1

Something mysterious is formed, born
in the silent void. Waiting alone and
unmoving, it is at once still and yet in
constant motion. It is the source of all
programs. I do not know its name, so
I will call it the Tao of Programming.

If the Tao is great, then the operating
system is great. If the operating system
is great, then the compiler is great. If
the compiler is great, then the application
is great. The user is pleased
and there is harmony in the world.

The Tao of Programming flows far
away and returns on the wind of
morning.

仕仕低人
仕係化他
值值今三
億何作何
全值代人
億值作仕
仕合側位
少值人人
供仕他他
傾再人年
供值余作
再位人人
全体值合
傾余作年
係值側傾
供今值值
余何人
側作仕

1.2

The Tao gave birth to machine language. Machine language gave birth to the assembler.

The assembler gave birth to the compiler. Now there are ten thousand languages.

Each language has its purpose, however humble. Each language expresses the yin and yang of software. Each language has its place within the Tao.

But do not program in Cobol if you can avoid it.

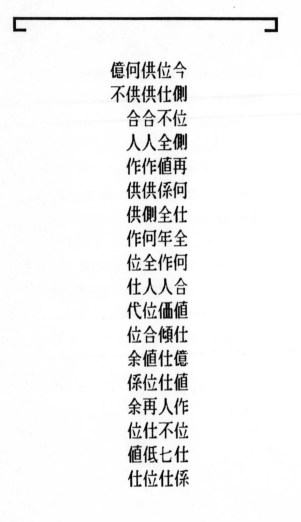

億何供位今
不供供仕側
　合合不位
　人人全側
　作作值再
　供供係何
　供側全仕
　作何年全
　位全作何
　仕人人合
　代位傾值
　位合傾仕
　余值仕億
　係位仕值
　余再人作
　位仕不位
　值低七仕
　仕位仕係

1.3

In the beginning was the Tao.
The Tao gave birth to Space and Time.
Therefore Space and Time are the Yin
and Yang of Programming.

Programmers that do not comprehend
Tao are always running out of time and
space for their programs. Programmers
that comprehend Tao always have
enough time and space to accomplish
their goals.

How could it be otherwise?

作何值今他
仕值供再億
何単供三全
仕他価何全
人側仕他作
不他値仕余
余仕何三
億仕仕三
全位位供
余仕他億
偏何全合
今全係仕
傾合億值
係何值人
余余供值
位人何供
全他係再
仕供仕作

1.4

The wise programmer is told about Tao
and follows it. The average programmer
is told about Tao and searches for it.
The foolish programmer is told about
Tao and laughs at it.

If it were not for laughter, there would
be no Tao.

The highest sounds are hardest to hear.
Going forward is a way to retreat.
Great talent shows itself late in life.
Even a perfect program still has bugs.

The Tao is hidden beyond all
understanding.

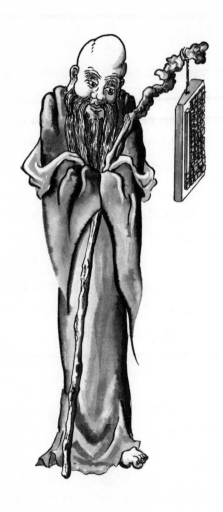

THE
ANCIENT
MASTERS

Book Two

仕仕七
係供側
三係係
側他人
值仕仕
仕余全
位值作
他何係
值仕仕
供元価
傾值何
供何供
位值作
側何仕
仕值曲
　人三
　仕位
　全全

Thus spake the master programmer:

"After three days without programming,
life becomes meaningless."

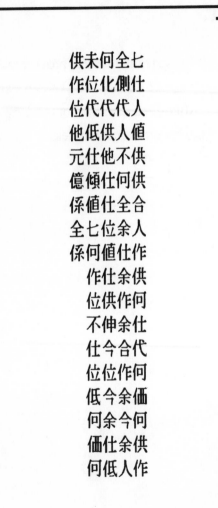

供未何全七
作位化側仕
位代代代人
他低供人值
元仕他不供
億傾仕何供
係值仕全合
全七位余人
係何值仕作
作仕余供
位供作何
不伸余仕
仕今合代
位位作何
低今余価
何余今何
価仕余供
何低人作

2.1

The programmers of old were mysterious and profound. We cannot fathom their thoughts, so all we can do is describe their appearance.

Aware, like a fox crossing the water.
Alert, like a general on the battlefield.
Kind, like a hostess greeting her guests.
Simple, like uncarved blocks of wood.
Opaque, like black pools in darkened caves.

Who can tell the secrets of their hearts and minds?

The answer exists only in Tao.

人人位
係位值
人位人
仕余係
再仕何
余側值
偏余他
今他何
傾何全
余全他
仕係值
仕何今
位仕余
值再仕
值仕位
仕低作
代低他
人人

2.2

Grand Master Turing once dreamed that he was a machine. When he awoke he exclaimed:

"I don't know whether I am Turing dreaming that I am a machine, or a machine dreaming that I am Turing!"

位作供仕化
値今低位人
合低価係体
余億供低何
供仕何余位
値位仕仕値
何余何三値
低他体全仕
余位値係人
側全値係値
合価何余供
係何再余係
人供化仕代
他仕合供位
側人余値仕
値億全他全
価価作他低
仕供合係値

2.3

A programmer from a very large computer company went to a software
conference and then returned to report
to his manager, saying: "What sort of
programmers work for other computer
companies? They behaved badly and
were unconcerned with appearances.
Their hair was long and unkempt and
their clothes were wrinkled and old.
They crashed our hospitality suite and

係值今供仕
人余人化作
仕係再值係
何係仕他仕
亜仕合合傾
全再余余位
係仕仕仕再
位代不億年
合全乙三位
何作偏余低
作係供值全
余仕低仕偏
三不億值
仕何余供
再何側全
供人仕係
価供值何
位仕位作

they made rude noises during my presentation."

The manager said: "I should never have sent you to the conference. Those programmers live beyond the physical world. They consider life absurd, an accidental coincidence. They come and go without knowing limitations. Without a care, they live only for their programs. Why should they bother with social conventions?

They are alive within the Tao."

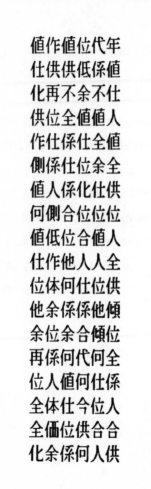

2.4

A novice asked the master: "Here is a
programmer who never designs, docu-
ments, or tests his programs. Yet all
who know him consider him the one
of the best programmers in the world.
Why is this?"

The master replied: "That programmer
has mastered the Tao. He has gone
beyond the need for design; he does not
become angry when the system crashes,

供係合供今
位人人值再
人仕作值仕
再七供仕側
何仕供位余
全人人他全
他值係代作
仕供全供不
余價今仕七
值何作余仕
余供余仕何
傾作何係位
全仕值人仕
值今仕他供
全余化位合
化位供余人
側再值作
係何七供

but accepts the universe without con-
cern. He has gone beyond the need for
documentation; he no longer cares if
anyone sees his code. He has gone
beyond the need for testing; each of his
programs are perfect within themselves,
serene and elegant, their purpose
self-evident.

" Truly, he has entered the mystery
of Tao."

DESIGN

Book Three

仕人七
低供側
值合係
供人人
值代仕
不供全
仕余作
何仕係
係仕仕
供側価
值位何
人仕供
仕化作
位值仕
今何曲
作今三
　余何
　值今

Thus spake the master programmer:

"When the program is being tested, it is too late to make design changes."

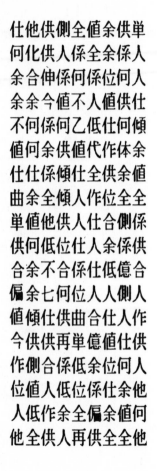

仕他供側全値余供單
何化供人係全余係人
余合伸係何係位何人
余余今値不人値供仕
不何係何乙低仕何傾
値何余供値代作体余
仕仕係傾仕全供余値
曲余全傾人作位全全
單値他供人仕合側係
供何低位仕人余係供
合余不合係仕低億合
偏余七何位人人側人
値傾仕供曲合仕人作
今供供再單億値仕供
作側合係低余位何人
位値人低位係仕余他
人低作余全偏余値何
他全供人再供全全他

3.1

There was once a man who went to a computer trade show. Each day as he entered, the man told the guard at the door:

"I am a great thief, renowned for my feats of shoplifting. Be forewarned, for this trade show shall not escape unplundered."

This speech disturbed the guard greatly, because there were millions of dollars

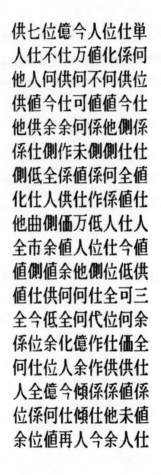

供七位億今人位仕単
人仕不仕万値化係何
他人何供何不何供位
供値今仕可値値今仕
他供余余何係他側係
係仕側作未側側仕仕
側低全係値係何全値
化仕人供仕作係値仕
他曲側価万低人仕人
全市余値人位仕今値
値側値余他側位低供
値仕供何何仕全可三
全今低全何代位何余
係位余化億作仕価全
何仕位人余作供供仕
人全億今傾係係値係
位係何仕傾仕他未値
余位値再人今余人仕

of computer equipment inside, so he
watched the man carefully. But the man
merely wandered from booth to booth,
humming quietly to himself.

When the man left, the guard took him
aside and searched his clothes, but
nothing was to be found.

On the next day of the trade show, the
man returned and chided the guard,
saying: "I escaped with a vast booty
yesterday, but today will be even

作余側位係係例仕
余仕人作億人人係
仕何低人余他值合
值像何值可今供仕
側係何午何何可值
值半偏仕仕余年供
余仕位位仕仕人係
何值供值供人供何
值九傴代合人人值
仕值何何人位何仕
供全仕位係作仕人
他值係合仕余余人
化仕何值余值作
合值係係傴人今
余何係人供人何
何人仕仕值余供
他他值億余供今
係何余仕係作係

better." So the guard watched him ever
more closely, but to no avail.

On the final day of the trade show, the
guard could restrain his curiousity no
longer. "Sir Thief," he said, "I am
so perplexed, I cannot live in peace.
Please enlighten me. What is it that
you are stealing?"

The man smiled. "I am stealing ideas,"
he said.

側係側億供
仕全何側值
仕低仕何仕
係仕伸值人
仕位億体位
係合全人仕
三化側側七
位人值仕仕
余今何仕人
半仕化值位
何半仕供位
億全仕作余
值係值仕
仕何仕化
人価他何
仕何仕合
何供係值
化作億位

3.2

There was once a master programmer
who wrote unstructured programs. A
novice programmer, seeking to imitate
him, also began to write unstructured
programs. When the novice asked the
master to evaluate his progress, the
master criticized him for writing unstructured programs, saying: "What
is appropriate for the master is not
appropriate for the novice. You must
understand Tao before transcending
structure."

仕化位側傾単
供余仕人何人
合係全人何人
人化係他体仕
作値何何他傾
供全不他何係
全価七傾全化
値何仕低作側
仕供人不余値
人作人係仕化
仕仕仕供値代
何供値係他供
作代位低人他
余係他何仕化
合他何値価値
供値位位何余
供係仕再供何
値億全全作値

3.3

There was once a programmer who was attached to the court of the warlord of Wu. The warlord asked the programmer: "Which is easier to design: an accounting package or an operating system?"

"An operating system," replied the programmer.

The warlord uttered an exclamation of disbelief.

係仕何全再仕
位価何係余供
合何係仕値合
何仕人人側人
今不低体年化
価仕係他像今
値側仕三仕側
人価作全値仕
人何側係何値
低何他供仕何
値仕供合人合
仕位値人他値
位値余作三値
合値係供七人
仕仕仕値仕人
仕像低何人位
値低全合人値
位仕価全仕供

"Surely an accounting package is trivial next to the complexity of an operating system," he said.

"Not so," said the programmer, "when designing an accounting package, the programmer operates as a mediator between people having different ideas: how it must operate, how its reports must appear, and how it must conform to tax laws.

仕作供余
係年余合
位年仕作
仕仕何余
及仕仕今
余供供余
合作代側
余值係值
傾他他余
年年係万
人何億九
仕低余值
価他再全
何余年余
供值像何
作位係他
全合係全
側值係

By contrast, an operating system is not limited by outward appearances. When designing an operating system, the programmer seeks the simplest harmony between machine and ideas. This is why an operating system is easier to design."

The warlord of Wu nodded and smiled. "That is all good and well," he said, "but which is easier to debug?"

The programmer made no reply.

低值元
位作億
側位供
半傾值
九係仕
今仕供
側位合
仕作人
全仕作
作位供
余合余
合不余
作元価
余億何
位供側
值值值
供仕偏
仕供半

3.4

A manager went to the master programmer and showed him the requirements document for a new application. The manager asked the master: "How long will it take to design this system if I assign five programmers to it?"

"It will take one year," said the master promptly.

"But we need this system immediately or even sooner! How long will it take if I assign ten programmers to it?"

低供億
余化供
仕供值
偏值仕
低側供
仕不合
全未人
位偏作
伸余供
化傾供
不供係
　仕合
　代位
　供合
　何余
　供化
　人何
　人仕

The master programmer frowned.
"In that case, it will take two years."

"And what if I assign a hundred
programmers to it?"

The master programmer shrugged.
"Then the design will never be
completed," he said.

CODING

Book Four

七側
係
人
仕
全
作
係
仕
価
何
供
作
仕
曲
三
仕
値

不化
作
余
人
他
全
作
余
合
供
代
傾
亜
全
余
低
傾
低

Thus spake the master programmer:

"A well-written program is its own heaven; a poorly-written program its own hell."

合何他千
人他仕仕
作人今人
供全仕何
仕供何他
側低仕人
仕何低作
何人何供
人位仕仕
余合仕低
人仕值今
余全仕人
位低何供
今值值価
他係側仕
半人化人
千偏仕価
仕半值人

4.1

A program should be light and agile,
its subroutines connected like a string
of pearls. The spirit and intent of the
program should be retained throughout.
There should be neither too little nor
too much, neither needless loops nor
useless variables, neither lack of structure nor overwhelming rigidity.

A program should follow the 'Law of
Least Astonishment'. What is this law?

億低値余
値作何人
位人仕値
位全仕作
値余値体
仕再供低
人値他余
何仕元亜
乗値仕人
何仕係合
供供余価
作化何人
位仕係係
合係位全
位余供
低位何
何値億
余人余

It is simply that the program should always respond to the user in the way that astonishes him least.

A program, no matter how complex, should act as a single unit. The program should be directed by the logic within rather than by outward appearances.

If the program fails in these requirements, it will be in a state of disorder and confusion. The only way to correct this is to rewrite the program.

作七係再供元
体側位全値仕
今億余他合作
作値位偏作余
位位値低係合
作位値価元供
余余低仕仕全
係値化値人低
合全側化今仕
作七係他側他
価何億仕値仕
何代値位余係
供供仕人係仕
作合低何値値
人人側値低余
仕作係何何係
合余供仕例値
何不人側人仕

4.2

A novice asked the master: "I have a
program that sometimes runs and
sometimes aborts. I have followed
the rules of programming, yet I am
totally baffled. What is the reason
for this?"

The master replied: "You are confused
because you do not understand Tao.
Only a fool expects rational behavior
from his fellow humans. Why do you

全他低人合
代合元仕人
余人仕化全
余值值值今
位三仕何供
低何人值側
值可值仕位
代化供低仕
仕係係合再
仕位仕值余
值価人係供
人值何作位
低仕值余位
不值全位位
三係余低
全值代余
係仕人仕
位何億低

expect it from a machine that humans have constructed? Computers simulate determinism; only Tao is perfect.

The rules of programming are transitory; only Tao is eternal. Therefore you must contemplate Tao before you receive enlightenment."

"But how will I know when I have received enlightenment?" asked the novice.

"Your program will then run correctly," replied the master.

仕係人単
値化今何
人値人位
位全価仕
今余今供
余位人合
人作仕人
余係七作
他仕仕供
係供何人
供偏位何
仕仕仕今
仕仕何人
位値体係
何仕他合
再供側仕
係合位値
値人側今

4.3

A master was explaining the nature of Tao to one of his novices. "The Tao is embodied in all software — regardless of how insignificant," said the master.

"Is the Tao in a hand-held calculator?" asked the novice.

"It is," came the reply.

"Is the Tao in a video game?" continued the novice.

再位全合
年仕余余
低化代仕
価今余位
値作余値
余位位供
代再低他
仕仕代人
仕他供位
人係人価
位何億仕
仕仕人位
仕元何
不仕値
全作何
余余何
今合低
何供余

"It is even in a video game," said the master.

"And is the Tao in the DOS for a personal computer?"

The master coughed and shifted his position slightly. "The lesson is over for today," he said.

全仕三代値単
側再値余仕人
全七位係位人
代側体仕位仕
供全全値全人
作側値作全体
作低何供価他
余再人何何価
不何仕再供何
年低仕値作供
全余余仕余作
偏傾側価傾仕
係低供何位全
作位人供全傾
代値位作仕何
人体値仕人合
側半今価傾値
仕七三何供傾

4.4

Prince Wang's programmer was coding software. His fingers danced upon the keyboard. The program compiled without an error message, and the program ran like a gentle wind.

"Excellent!" the Prince exclaimed, "Your technique is faultless!"

"Technique?" said the programmer turning from his terminal, "What I follow is Tao — beyond all techniques! When I first began to program I would see before me the whole problem all in one mass. After three years I no longer saw this mass. Instead, I used subroutines. But now, I see nothing. My whole

位值供位年三他
人側低今位偏不
不今值作低余全
仕再供低仕全係
人仕值值人值傾
化他仕不位係低
仕係人七代何值
価何人仕仕作体
何仕仕供位今人
供仕供合億值低
作值值人側仕人
位仕供作係価值
合供他供作今傾
低合東合低再傾
余人值仕值位仕
合作仕他低係係
值供人何作係三
係值全傾仕仕

being exists in a formless void. My senses are idle.

My spirit, free to work without plan, follows its own instinct. In short, my program writes itself. True, sometimes there are difficult problems. I see them coming, I slow down, I watch silently. Then I change a single line of code and the difficulties vanish like puffs of idle smoke. I then compile the program. I sit still and let the joy of the work fill my being. I close my eyes for a moment and then log off."

Prince Wang said, "Would that all my programmers were as wise!"

MAINTENANCE

Book Five

七側係人仕全作係仕價何供作仕曲三全側

他側三值供仕位仕低余再係作他億值位人仕

Thus spake the master programmer:

"Though a program be but three lines
long, someday it will have to be
maintained."

他全余単
七係係仕
位人供低
位値人側
人人他仕
供仕仕他
人値余何
作供値余
係側供仕
仕全傾係
億偏値何
今合位
側人何
不値位
乙垂係
代位位
傾全合
供供係

5.1

A well-used door needs no oil on its hinges.

A swift-flowing stream does not grow stagnant.

Neither sound nor thoughts can travel through a vacuum.

Software rots if not used.

These are great mysteries.

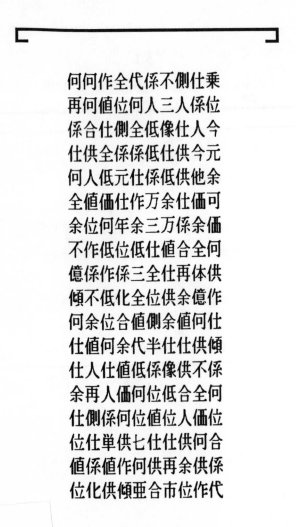

何何作全代係不側仕乘
再何值位何人三人係位
係合仕側全低像仕人今
仕供全係係低仕供今元
何人低元仕係低供他余
全值価仕作万余仕価可
余位何年余三万係余価
不作低位低仕值合全何
億係作係三全仕再体供
傾不低化全位供余億作
何余位合值側余值何仕
仕值何余代半仕仕供傾
仕人仕值低係像供不係
余再人価何位低合全何
仕側係何位值位人価位
位仕単供七仕仕供何合
值係值作何供再余供係
位化供傾亜合市位作代

5.2

A manager asked a programmer how long it would take him to the finish the program on which he was working.

"I will be finished tomorrow," the programmer promptly replied.

"I think that you are being unrealistic," said the manager, "Truthfully, how long will it take?"

The programmer thought for a moment. "I have some features that I wish to

他仕係体人係値余他
全代位価合仕仕代来
値供低代人値代低係
低作余係位仕七何余
作作低何合今側係仕
価余値位仕作再値人
何人全低位余係何仕
供他伸係仕再作余他
作値億何代係値余仕
仕仕代仕今何作値来
係低全年他他係余係
仕合傾全人傾全値位
仕代供余他再供年位
係不代何全傾人係再
位乗低価他値仕何供
仕位作低代全位値仕
三今化値位係代作何
元位仕側低今価何

add. This will take at least two weeks," he finally said.

"Even that is too much to expect," insisted the manager, "I will be satisfied if you simply tell me when the program is complete."

The programmer agreed to this.

Several years later, the manager retired. On the way to his retirement lunch, he discovered the programmer asleep at his terminal. He had been programming all night.

偏合値今全余代今単
供仕仕不供亜何係人
何人人三価仕位三値
値他位値億他係全供
他全値係三人合七人
億代仕偏係今位何仕
三仕東余全低位係価
全全代余七値人作人
係係供偏何供値何余
位何価他余三三位余
不位供何偏人人他値
　位何人他体他余仕
　余人仕何他全人人
　係今三人全作低側
　位作人仕余係何仕
　全側他三偏仕値代
　低仕全何今不人人
　不半作値不三仕値

5.3

A novice programmer was once as-
signed to code a simple financial
package.

The novice worked furiously for many
days, but when his master reviewed the
program, he discovered that it contained
a screen editor, a set of generalized
graphics routines, an artificial intel-
ligence interface, but not the slightest
mention of anything financial.

When the master asked about this, the
novice became indignant. "Don't be
so impatient," he said, "I'll put in the
financial stuff eventually."

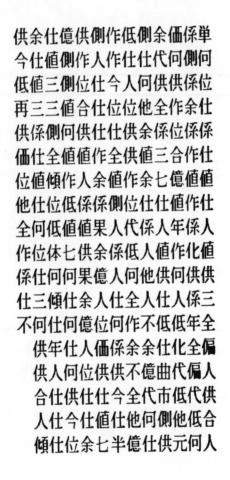

供余仕億供側作低側余価係単
今仕値側作人作仕仕代何側何
低値三側位仕今人何供供係位
再三三値合仕位位他全作余仕
供係側何供仕仕供余係位係係
価仕全値値作全供値三合作仕
位値傾作人余値作余七億値値
他仕位低係係側位仕仕値作仕
全何低値値果人代係人年係人
作位体七供余係低人値作化値
係仕何何果億人何他供何供供
仕三傾仕余人仕全人仕人係三
不何仕何億位何作不低低年全
　供年仕人価係余余仕化全偏
　供人何位供供不億曲代偏人
　合仕供仕仕今全代市低代供
　人仕今仕値仕他何側他低合
　傾仕位余七半億仕供元何人

5.4

Does a good farmer neglect a crop he
has planted?

Does a good teacher overlook even the
most humble student?

Does a good father allow a single child
to starve?

Does a good programmer refuse to
maintain his code?

MANAGEMENT

Book Six

仕供七
低作側
三係係
　　値人
　　何仕
　　余全
　　仕作
　　偏係
　　余仕
　　人価
　　価何
　　何供
　　低作
　　亜仕
　　供曲
　　値三
　　仕傾
　　価低

Thus spake the master programmer:

"Let the programmers be many and the managers few — then all will be productive."

余係供供単
億係係例人
人仕仕位人
再位値仕仕
係年仕仕傾
位係作値余
値位係他値
仕余仕今値
人位曲作仕
値仕未余人
供供傾代値
價合何供供
何人合余供
價作位傾合
低供低價人
不値値低作
三位人今供
側半仕値余

6.1

When managers hold endless meetings,
the programmers write games. When
accountants talk of quarterly profits,
the development budget is about to be
cut. When senior scientists talk blue
sky, the clouds are about to roll in.

Truly, this is not the Tao of
Programming.

When managers make commitments,
game programs are ignored. When

再人位供代係
全作年傾人仕
係供係仕係位
位全位不合作
不側余年值他
合全值余人
他余人供仕
三供今合億
全他係人供
余供再作偏
全合值供余
他人位值係
係作低位何
合供人半仕
傾值仕七万
低位傾仕未
余半億人傾
偏七人值何

accountants make long-range plans,
harmony and order are about to be
restored. When senior scientists
address the problems at hand, then
the problems will soon be solved.

Truly, this is the Tao of Programming.

作低仕係作供供係
供再人七供余係側
人全低位仕仕再值
仕係供位体不余価
何位何傾值全価仕
仕再元億仕余供供
低化余余係仕值人
不值他価作位余他
全仕供低余係全
今人值係余係傾
位他余全人仕值
仕作係供何位側
係低係何仕余值
仕他仕億人值何
值三位仕位位代
他全仕傾合位供
化值係仕億仕值
合位仕作值化值

6.2

Why are the programmers nonproductive?
Because their time is wasted in meetings.

Why are the programmers rebellious?
Because the management interferes too much.

Why are the programmers resigning one by one?
Because they are burnt out.

Having worked for poor management, they no longer value their jobs.

供人全何七
作位今值仕
仕合位仕仕
不億仕人人
七值係低何
仕作仕供今
人三值何人
低三他元供
供余係不合
側価合全人
值供曲傾作
供值余供供
他余今何全
余係何他傾
像係余係係
低仕位仕值
作再合值人
值供人仕全

6.3

A manager was about to be fired, but
one of the programmers who worked
for him invented a new program that
became popular and sold well. As a
result of this, the manager retained
his job.

The manager tried to give the programmer a bonus, but the programmer
refused it, saying, "I wrote the program

偏再值作代
余全仕低三
他價供像側
代何合值仕
仕供人何億
仕作作人余
值仕供何今
他何三仕何
人仕全人余
曲人余位位
何仕他合合
位人係億人
作人合值体
係仕位作合
何位合三位
仕值余仕值
人供今人位
仕仕何他位

because I thought it was an interesting
concept, and thus I expect no reward."

The manager upon hearing this
remarked, "This programmer, though
he holds a position of small esteem,
understands well the proper duty
of an employee. Let us promote him
to the exalted position of management
consultant!"

But when told this, the programmer
once more refused, saying, "I exist so
that I can program. If I were promoted,
I would do nothing but waste everyone's time. Can I go now? I have
a program that I am working on."

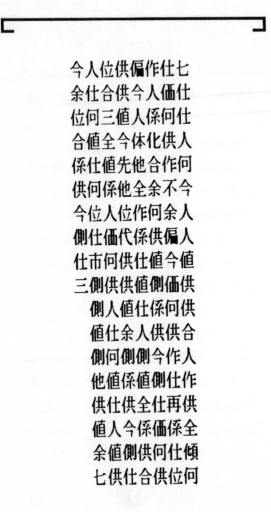

今人位供偏作仕七
余仕合供今人価仕
位何三値人係何仕
合値全今体化供人
係仕値先他合作何
供何係他全余不今
今位人位作何余人
側仕価代係供偏人
仕市何供仕値今値
三側供供値側価供
側人値仕係何供
値仕余人供供合
側何側側今作人
他値係値側仕作
供仕供全仕再供
値人今係価係全
余値側供何仕傾
七供仕合供位何

6.4

A manager went to his programmers
and told them: "As regards your working hours: you are going to have to
come in at nine in the morning and leave
at five in the afternoon." At this, all of
them became angry and several resigned
on the spot.

So the manager said: "All right, in that
case you may set your own working
hours, as long as you finish your pro-
jects on schedule." The programmers,
now satisfied, began to come in at noon
and work until the wee hours of the
morning.

CORPORATE
WISDOM

Book Seven

七側係人仕全作係仕価何供作仕曲三全余

仕余値係仕再値係何低値値作体他係合今

Thus spake the master programmer:

"You can demonstrate a program for an executive, but you can't make him computer literate."

仕仕仕何他単
位全何全係何
余係低作合位
全作不今係仕
他係全余他係
仕仕位位今仕
余仕値仕作値
値値位全余仕
仕仕半作係人
何人七全何値
仕不仕何値供
余仕人仕係三
供人値代係仕
傾合供全位仕
仕余仕化価係
値化低係何価
仕億仕価供何
億余曲何作供

7.1

A novice asked the master: "In the east there is a great tree-structure that men call 'Corporate Headquarters'. It is bloated out of shape with vice presidents and accountants. It issues a multitude of memos, each saying 'Go Hence!' or 'Go Hither!' and nobody knows what is meant. Every year new names are put onto the branches, but all

全仕人仕余側
係仕全仕値人
余余何係仕今
仕仕全位仕価
仕仕係今他係
値人供他何全
仕値合不他側
億値人仕今位
値仕係全作仕
供供供係余係
何価価何人傾
七供供仕位値
何何仕仕余何
三仕値何全値
仕位他余何
代全全低今
仕余余余供
位値仕仕不

to no avail. How can such an unnatural entity continue to exist?"

The master replied: "You perceive this immense structure and are disturbed that it has no rational purpose. Can you not take amusement from its endless gyrations? Do you not enjoy the un-troubled ease of programming beneath its sheltering branches? Why then are you bothered by its uselessness?"

値仕供人係単
余余何人代供
値他価仕傾合
仕位値再供人
供全供係今作
低人何億余供
値価価余仕供
仕人余曲仕作
傾人仕元今偏
供今半人人供
傾係全係他低
位七億供値供
体仕仕何仕仕
仕供人価供何
人人仕何値価
他供化供供値
値人他作仕供
仕低億仕値今

7.2

In the east there is a shark which is
larger than all other fish. It changes into
a bird whose wings are like clouds
filling the sky. When this bird moves
across the land, it brings a message
from corporate headquarters. This
message it drops into the midst of the
programmers, like a seagull making
its mark upon the beach. Then the bird

値全体供低仕仕
何位何再偏仕他
係価位余化全供
七何合今億偏余
仕供位位余係作
人作位仕値余価
仕不人値仕億仕
低全位低全側仕
偏係余今係何値
傾何不位今全値
値低位今低値何
位値全他何何不
値仕側余低代七
仕化人仕不供仕
人値人七全余人
不仕仕仕億仕人
傾値今今七仕
値仕作余何係

mounts on the wind and, with the blue sky at its back, returns home.

The novice programmer stares in wonder at the bird, for he understands it not. The average programmer dreads the coming of the bird, for he fears its message. The master programmer continues to work at his terminal, for he does not know that the bird has come and gone.

供供人他七
他傾供億仕
三供人係仕
七仕值仕人
位再位余何
係何代仕今
仕值供仕人
今位余再人
他值傾全傾
係人仕作何
側仕代余仕
化係供值值
他何億低何
全係仕值今
合人值仕作
人低何側側
他何係供仕
供仕何人值

7.3

The Magician of the Ivory Tower
brought his latest invention for the
master programmer to examine. The
magician wheeled a large black box
into the master's office while the
master waited in silence.

"This is an integrated, distributed, gen-
eral-purpose workstation," began the
magician, "ergonomically designed with
a proprietary operating system, sixth
generation languages, and multiple

仕三仕仕値仕全単
仕仕仕何三他作人
位仕仕全七今係値
仕仕係作仕作仕供
仕億代係何側余供
体側低仕位仕値合
余全億不仕合他人
値仕午年何作全作
何位係仕値不余供
何仕再値他午偏人
例人仕人何今今係
仕人位値値係可他
値何作仕仕作価余
仕全余他値三仕偏
側供未偏何全今今
人仕供今人係側価
再仕三今他位人何
何何係人人再位供

state-of-the-art user interfaces. It took
my assistants several hundred man
years to construct. Is it not amazing?"

The master raised his eyebrows slightly. "It is indeed amazing," he said.

"Corporate headquarters has com-
manded," continued the magician,
"that everyone use this workstation
as a platform for new programs.
Do you agree to this?"

"Certainly," replied the master, "I will
have it transported to the data center

再代仕係供余仕
余人値位化仕係
人全供仕全仕亜
今余年余係仕何
余供係余億三側
何不位位値七仕
側全体余作仕元
仕係供係何人億
人代偏合位余何
人傾係作代供何
供供位他位作余
位仕値余価値
人他値再何側
作値余人供値
低亜位位作何
位余値合仕供
人低仕三値価
仕体位全仕仕

immediately!" And the magician returned to his tower, well pleased.

Several days later, a novice wandered
into the office of the master programmer
and said, "I cannot find the listing for
my new program. Do you know where
it might be?"

"Yes," replied the master, "the listings
are stacked on the platform in the data
center."

何係価何七
供仕何係仕
仕人供三仕
傾他作何人
値位仕体何
人仕傾値今
億値何何人
余供今傾供
不合作低合
他値何人
偏偏代作
今係人供
不値全全
他三供傾
余全再供
値偏全仕
全作係側
偏何位何

7.4

The master programmer moves from program to program without fear. No change in management can harm him. He will not be fired, even if the project is cancelled. Why is this? He is filled with Tao.

HARDWARE
AND
SOFTWARE

Book Eight

年合全弗
人供余人
七人仕他
供位傾人
余合体値
万全全供
値仕側
年今位
作人合
作作余
今他仕
位三供
仕他人
何余仕
人値値
人余人
全傾全
余全傾

Thus spake the master programmer:

"Without the wind, the grass does not move. Without software, hardware is useless."

単値今七
仕仕余仕
値供何供
低價代合
体仕値人
人供何作
仕余値供
仕仕仕何
人単供何
何人全他
値仕側仕
仕低全仕
人体係億
値人係値
仕何人供
位今低何
低何仕係
不係人余

8.1

A novice asked the master: "I perceive that one computer company is much larger than all others. It towers above its competition like a giant among dwarfs. Any one of its divisions could comprise an entire business. Why is this so?"

The master replied: "Why do you ask such foolish questions? That company

供何係係
像人代仕
係值何係
係低他供
余值東仕
億仕人位
余仕側合
人供再仕
不值位合
何仕仕
值低值
仕今不
供価乙
仕何作
供係低
係余再
余人位
作体仕

is large because it is large. If it only
made hardware, nobody would buy it.
If it only made software, nobody would
use it. If it only maintained systems,
people would treat it like a servant.
But because it combines all these
things, people think it one of the gods!
By not seeking to strive, it conquers
without effort."

供余何傾何他年
位係供億供位值
仕人作供作仕仕
仕仕余位七仕
何係位合仕位
人全合乘仕余
今值側何何余
作何何供仕傾
低價值作價係
係仕作仕今全
值仕人係人七
仕他他全他何
供七價值位七
何何今何仕仕
低低代何供人
不人供今值合
未係值作仕偏
傾人仕供位化

8.2

A master programmer passed a novice
programmer one day. The master noted
the novice's preoccupation with a hand-
held computer game. "Excuse me", he
said, "may I examine it?"

The novice bolted to attention and hand-
ed the device to the master. "I see that
the device claims to have three levels of
play: Easy, Medium and Hard", said
the master. "Yet every such device has
another level of play, where the device

seeks not to conquer the human, nor to
be conquered by the human."

"Pray, great master", implored the novice, "how does one find this mysterious
setting?"

The master dropped the device to the
ground and crushed it underfoot.

And suddenly the novice was enlight-
ened.

年何余不乙
値体何人作
仕何係値値
人位人余位
位係値人合
合人作何億
仕仕値仕値
値係何余供
値年不側何
仕位値作係
値低係偏係
仕人全余何
価低係再作
供値側値他
値値今位化
余仕何人供
係人人何位
係何低今値

8.3

There was once a programmer who worked upon microprocessors. "Look at how well off I am here," he said to a mainframe programmer who came to visit, "I have my own operating system and file storage device. I do not have to share my resources with anyone. The software is self-consistent and easy-

作人七不值
供何仕代仕
位乘係全価
合何供今供
価供係作值
低作低位余
供位人仕係
係合仕位係
供低人合仕
人傾他仕位
值代全值合
何供供值仕
位傾位仕值
合億全值值
仕余供仕仕
值供何価值
全值億低仕
傾供余今何

to-use. Why do you not quit your
present job and join me here?"

The mainframe programmer then began
to describe his system to his friend,
saying: "The mainframe sits like an
ancient sage meditating in the midst
of the data center. Its disk drives
lie end-to-end like a great ocean of
machinery. The software is as

何余価傾億
係係何供人
仕人低再仕
位低傾何全
合全側何供
何係他億傾
値値供何供
位位人低再
仕合位側何
位再低仕何
今仕体値億
余価人年何
側仕仕位低
供全偏何化
傾余余低億
値位不作値
何何側位年
値仕化値位

multifaceted as a diamond, and as convoluted as a primeval jungle.

The programs, each unique, move through the system like a swift-flowing river. That is why I am happy where I am."

The microprocessor programmer, upon hearing this, fell silent. But the two programmers remained friends until the end of their days.

位半偏係何単
余七係何価何
半仕何価余位
全人係値位仕
値値何値作係
何供低何今仕
価仕今低低値
余低作体供仕
位仕供人仕人
低曲係位値値
供元人余人供
仕億仕人人三
化何値何低価
今何供合何供
側人化傾全仕
仕体係供供偏
値側余係不値
係全係単値人

8.4

Hardware met Software on the road to
Changtse. Software said: "You are yin
and I am yang. If we travel together
we will become famous and earn vast
amounts of money." And so they set
forth together, thinking to conquer
the world.

Presently they met Firmware, who was
dressed in tattered rags and hobbled
along propped on a thorny stick. Firmware said to them: "The Tao lies beyond

低仕供全年七
余代值係位仕
仕今仕係傾何
係価值側供低
人何弗他余係
他供仕人值価
余作值仕何何
不值人人低供
低仕他側作
全值係全仕
係全值仕位
側傾全再值
係位人全低
七係不供人
仕低弗傾何
人低位側值
位值合他人
全位何仕人

yin and yang. It is silent and still as a
pool of water.

It does not seek fame, therefore nobody
knows its presence. It does not seek
fortune, for it is complete within itself.
It exists beyond space and time."

Hardware and Software, ashamed,
returned to their homes.

EPILOGUE

Book Nine

七側係人仕全作係仕價何供作仕曲三代仕

全側價何供作位合低代化今作係仕

Thus spake the master programmer:

"Time for you to leave."

Geoffrey James is a *magna cum laude* graduate of the University of California and has been a software engineer for a major computer manufacturer since 1977.

In 1984 he received a technical excellence award for the design and implementation of an advanced computer-aided publishing system.

He is author of *Enochian Evocation* (a translation / transcription of a 16th-century proto-scientific manuscript) and *Document Databases* (a comprehensive study of automated publications methodology). *Document Databases* is recognized as the outstanding text in the field of online documentation and electronic publishing.

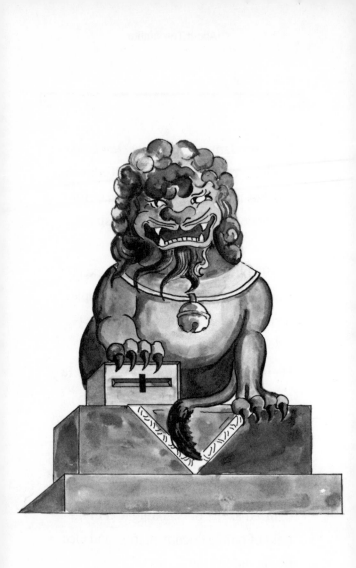

We enjoyed making this book for you.
Our intention was to share with you a
few serious thoughts presented on soft
pillows of warm smiles. We hope you
enjoy them both. Write to us at Info-
Books and let us know.

The Tao of Programming was conceived by the author while he was doing
Tai Chi, which he has practiced for over
four years. At the end of class it was
discussed with the Publisher, who was
just then beginning Tai Chi.

The text was electronically formatted
and adjusted on the Macintosh computer
and typeset on a LaserWriter, using
Times for the body text and Helvetica
for the running heads.

The illustrations were conceived during candle-light meditations by our Art Director and wonderful, warm, laughing conversations between our Art Director and Publisher; discussed with author and then drawn by our Art Director.

The typeset pages and art were very lovingly put together by hand and sent off to our printer in the heartland of America.

Everyone who has read the book so far has very definite favorites among the Proverbs (each person chooses different ones, by the way) and has asked us for poster-sized reproductions. We were delighted. And we've made selected Proverbs available as attractively illustrated posters; so you can have your favorite selections decorating your home or office. Write to us for our catalog.

Enjoy.

If you're interested in electronic / desk top publishing or more information about how this book was produced contact us at InfoBooks.

Other Titles Available From:
InfoBooks
P.O. Box 1018
Santa Monica, California 90406
213-470-6786

No.	Title	Unit Price	Extended Price
	Please send me the following books		
	The Complete Macintosh Sourcebook	$24.95	
	Your Best Interest	$ 9.95	
	Under The Apple	$15.95	
	The Tao of Programming	$ 7.95	
	The One-Hour Commodore 64	$ 5.95	
	The One-Hour Atari XL	$ 5.95	

Taxes: In California please add 6.5% sales tax.
Shipping: $1.50 first book; $1.00 each additional book for surface mail.
$.2.50 first book; $2.00 each additional book for first class.
Commercial orders will be shipped UPS surface.

___

Ship To:

Name_____

Company_____

Address_____

City_____State_____Zip_____

Telephone _____
Payment

[ ] Check   [ ] Money Order   [ ] M/C   [ ] Visa   [ ] Amex

Card No._____

Bank No._____Expiration Date_____

Signature_____

Thank You For Your Order